LOVE IN THE TIME OF CORONAVIRUS

A PANDEMIC PILGRIMAGE

ANGELA ALAIMO O'DONNELL

PARACLETE PRESS
BREWSTER, MASSACHUSETTS

For the many lost to Coronavirus
and those who love them,
For the many who have dedicated themselves
to the care and healing of the sick

Blessed are those who mourn
For they shall be comforted.
—Matthew 5:4

2021 First Printing

Love in the Time of Coronavirus: A Pandemic Pilgrimage

ISBN 978-1-64060-741-5

The Paraclete Press name and logo (dove on cross) are trademarks of Paraclete Press

Permission to use the cover image, *Room in New York*, Edward Hopper, 1932, was granted by Sheldon Museum of Art, University of Nebraska - Lincoln, Anna R. and Frank M. Hall Charitable Trust, H-166.1936

Library of Congress Control Number: 2021936212

10 9 8 7 6 5 4 3 2 1

Published by Paraclete Press
Brewster, Massachusetts
www.paracletepress.com

Printed in the United States of America

CONTENTS

III

IV

EPILOGUE

PROLOGUE

These poems map a private pilgrimage to nowhere—from the chair to the couch, the couch to the chair.

These poems also map a public pilgrimage through the landscape of pandemic, from dire disaster to the hope for healing.

They chronicle a year spent in lockdown in a small village just outside New York City. The lockdown was an unprecedented decree issued by the governor on March 22, 2020—a ruling that shut down the most populous city in America in an effort to stop the spread of the new Coronavirus that had arrived on our shores—or more precisely, in our airports—a few weeks before.

The lockdown was as total as it was sudden. Within a matter of days a State of Emergency was declared, the bustling theatres of Broadway went dark, New York City schools shut down, the city's many museums were closed, and thousands of bars and restaurants across the city and state were shuttered. Churches and synagogues were barred from holding services. Colleges and universities called a halt to in-person instruction and sent their students home. All sporting events, collegiate and professional, were cancelled. One of New York City's oldest and most enduring institutions, the St. Patrick's Day Parade, was called off the day before the event. It was then that we knew this was serious.

At the same time as the streets were emptying out, hospitals were filling up beyond capacity with the sick and the dying. Emergency Rooms were overrun. EMS responders were run ragged in a futile attempt to answer the thousands of calls they received. Sirens became the chronic and chaotic music of the city and its surrounding towns and villages. In one especially grim image that marks that early era, refrigerated trucks were brought in to hold the bodies of those who were dying in horrifying numbers.

Over the subsequent days and weeks, there were few pedestrians, fewer cars in the streets. Times Square, ordinarily the busiest spot in the city, grew eerily silent and empty, the enormous digital screens and billboards flashing and playing in their endless loop above the deserted sidewalks and intersections.

New Yorkers were urged to stay home. Only essential workers were supposed to be out and about. Many people began working from their homes and apartments. Zoom, a conference platform most of us had never heard of, became the lifeline to our livelihoods. People ordered groceries online, rather than braving the lines at Whole Foods and Gristedes. Families who lived in separate households did not visit each other for fear of catching and spreading the virus. Each of us felt our world become instantly contracted, shrunk down to the size of our house or apartment, perhaps our backyard if we were fortunate enough to have one.

Thus began the strangest year most of us had ever known. The virus and the subsequent lockdown touched and altered every aspect of our lives—who we saw and spoke to, what we ate and drank, where we went, when (if ever) we ventured out, how we conducted our daily routines. It became a time of intense and lamentable loneliness, isolation and alienation, terror and tragedy.

Yet for many of us, it also opened a door of opportunity. Released from the daily appointments, deadlines, and commutes that had formerly shaped our lives, we had the chance to choose how to spend our time. Time—that precious gift that had always seemed to be in such short supply—we suddenly had an abundance of, and we began to spend it in unaccustomed ways.

Lockdown offered us the experience of interiority, the chance to explore our own psyches, to become reacquainted with who we are when we aren't harried and hurried, living lives of busyness and distraction. In fact, the lockdown invited each of us to embark on an interior pilgrimage, a yearlong journey each of us had to take both alone and along with our friends, families, fellow New Yorkers, and fellow Americans.

It may seem a paradox to undertake a journey when one is confined to a single place, but, in reality, any pilgrimage worth making is a pilgrimage of the head and heart as much as it is one of the legs and feet. These poems attempt to capture this interior journey over the course of the year as we sheltered inside while the Coronavirus raged all around us. Written day by day, in response to the course of the virus and the attempts by public authorities to manage it, the poems chronicle events taking place in the macrocosm that shaped the experience of the microcosm—the little world I occupied from March 2020 to March 2021. While that world was entirely particular to me, it was also very much like the world(s) occupied by many other people, including the readers of these poems.

The title of the book, *Love in the Time of Coronavirus*, is borrowed from Gabriel Garcia Marquez's luminous novel *Love in the Time of Cholera*, about the enduring power of love in the face of time and deadly circumstance. This book of poems goes beyond Marquez's primary focus on romantic attachment to consider love in its many forms. As with Marquez's novel, these poems remind us that love flourishes even, and perhaps especially, during times of extremity, when the reality of mortality becomes palpable to us and we begin to see life in the context of eternity. It is then that love becomes the most powerful antidote we have to human suffering.

Living amid the Coronavirus catastrophe has occasioned extraordinary outpourings of love over the past year.

We have watched healthcare workers give of themselves without regard for their own safety, many of them risking their health and their lives in order to comfort and cure the afflicted.

We have seen frontline essential workers in service occupations courageously carrying out their duties—working in grocery stores and bodegas; delivering UPS, Fresh Direct, and endless Amazon orders; serving diners on patios once restaurants began to reopen.

We have witnessed people helping their sick and elderly neighbors and family members by shopping for them, delivering prepared meals, and picking up prescription medications.

We have heard of the endless hours public school teachers put in on Zoom, ministering to their students—and their parents—long after the official school day is over.

These are but a few of the many forms love has taken—and continues to take—during these late days of pandemic. These poems recognize this public love, a sign of our belief in the common good, as well as the many forms of private and personal love we practice—among them the uncountable emails, texts, social media posts, phone calls, and Zoom calls we share with our beloveds whom we are separated from, making ourselves present to them virtually when we cannot be present physically.

I think of these poems as one such expression of *Love in the Time of Coronavirus*. They constitute an offering, a series of singular moments pondered and shaped into poetic form—all of them sonnets, the pattern most suited to love—that coalesce into a shared history, a collective narrative of the rich and strange *Pandemic Pilgrimage* we have taken alone and together.

My hope is that readers might find in this book, despite the trials and privations of this pandemic year, some consolations, some moments of joy, some brief reminders that though the virus has robbed us of much, it cannot destroy the human capacity for love. To the contrary—miracle of miracles—it has enlarged it.

Angela Alaimo O'Donnell

ACKNOWLEDGMENTS

I wish to thank the editors of the following publications in which these poems have appeared or are forthcoming:

Angelus	"Transience"
Christian Century	"Covid Has Made Me Stupid"
	"Our Emmaus"
	"Super Moon"
Spiritus	"Wherein We Realize This Is Not Temporary"

I am grateful for the support of friends, editors, and fellow writers who have offered invaluable encouragement and support of these poems and this project, especially Mike Aquilina, Jill Peláez Baumgaertner, Mark Burrows, Ron Hansen, Paul Mariani, and John Poch.

I am especially grateful to my editor at Paraclete Press, Jon Sweeney, as well as to the Press and its excellent staff who designed and produced this book. Jon is a generous reader and a fine writer, and I am honored and delighted that he believed in these poems strongly enough to make them available to other readers.

Finally, as ever, I am grateful to my husband, Brennan, who has spent the past year in lockdown with me. We have made this Pandemic Pilgrimage together—a part of the lifelong pilgrimage we have been making for the past forty years. I could not wish for a better companion along the journey.

The Fire

The world is burning and we don't have a clue
how the fire started, when or where or who
lit the match and held it to the kindling trees,
watched the blaze blossom, set fire to the bees
who were too busy being to feel the heat
rising around them, devouring the flowers.
It took years, not months or weeks or hours
to lay it to waste. Every city and street
is a ghost town now. We haunt our own dreams.
The world as it used to be only seems—
impossibly green, sweet, blue, and true,
like a photo you took once, and now you
study to find yourself, trying to lay claim
to love before it went up in flame.

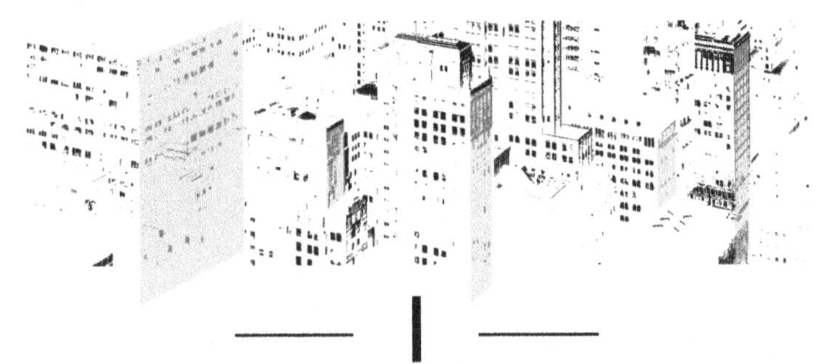

I

The Rules

March 22, 2020

Wash your hands while singing "Happy Birthday."
Touch nothing that's been touched by someone else.
Don't shake hands. Don't kiss. Don't touch yourself.
Don't travel anywhere. Just stop & stay
far & deep inside your own walls.
This way you won't bring it home with you.
Don't shop. Avoid the markets and malls.
The virus loves us all, Gentile and Jew,
the Buddhist, Baptist, pagan, Hindu—
each makes a fitting (if unwitting) host.
The preference it has is for the most
weak of us. He'll make a ghost of you
if you are old or ill. Better stay well,
young, and lonely in your chaste monk's cell.

Pandemic Music

Symphony of the garbage truck,
the bird chirp, the radiator.
New York City wakens to day
in the season of pandemic.
A little care and lots of luck
has spared us from the lung eater
so far. But we're academics.
We read all day about the way
people all around us die,
how small, malevolent, and sly
a virus we can't see can be.
We live our lives attentively.
The killer plague runs amok.
We listen for the garbage truck.

House Arrest

There's no place like home and home is no place
to hole up, day upon day upon day.
The hours tick by, stealthy and sly.
You never could read a clock face.
It tells a story of deceit.
You live this way, day upon day,
denying your inexorable defeat.
The window stares, the old couch bears
the burden of you with little grace.
The floorboards creak and do not care
who is awake and who sleeps.
It is a fact you need to face.
You would not learn it another way
but this one, day upon day upon day.

Covid Has Made Me Stupid

Good books line my shelves, but I don't read them.
Three sentences in and my mind wanders off
like a toddler in search of a snack. I stuff
her full of junk food—hours of CNN,
the Cuomo Boys, the president who pretends
to be the president while the rest of us
look away. Other offal she devours,
Culture Vulture, the *New York Times*, hours
after hours. She is starved and getting fat
on Facebook, Twitter, and Google Chat.
She ZOOMS all day on an empty tank.
Who do I blame for this, who do I thank
for ruining a perfectly fine brain?
I'll never write a poem again.

Time

Spend them well, your numbered days.
Let them go like aces
in a flush hand, with care
and attention. No fanfare
will sound as you lay your card
down on the table. Turn to face
your opponent, time. It's hard
to beat him, but there are ways

chief of which is enjoy the game,
hold lightly what you've got.
When he calls your bluff & your name
prove to him that you are not
the fool he is in your eyes.
Won't he be surprised.

Transience

What's here is here is here until it's not.
Your childhood home. The roses he brought.
Nothing is permanent as we think it is.
Nothing survives the last analysis.
All is contingent. Everything depends.
Everything begins & everything ends.
Clichés are just clichés until they come true.
Most tentative of all, me & you.

Nothing is permanent as we think it is.
What's mine isn't mine. What's his isn't his.
All is contingent. All of it depends.
You lose your lovers. You lose your friends.
The ripe piece of fruit will one day rot.
We're here and here and here until we're not.

In Praise of Food

Fat today because of Stuffed Peppers.
Browning the ground beef, tasting the sauce,
adding the parsley, the nutmeg and salt
enough to set my blood pressure roaring
through my sticky veins. Another supper
bigger than we need. It's not my fault
cooking calms me during a disaster,
an old skill I learned how to master
from childhood. My mother carried every cross
in her kitchen, drinking coffee, standing
at the stove, deciding what to make
to stave off sorrow—pasta, cookies, cake.
Some small good thing to feed the weary heart,
wake to a new day, practice her art.

In Which I Learn to Love My Neighbor

I love the lady who hands me my bread
when I go to the corner food store.
I love the man at the wine shop, who wipes
each bottle and tucks it in my sack.
I love the mailman, the UPS guy
who brings me things from the wide wide world
and sets them outside my front porch door.
I pray that none of them ends up dead
as they risk themselves daily for my sake.
So that I might eat, that I might have more
wine than I need, clothes I can't wear.
Such kindnesses stand between us and despair.
We who've neglected each other so long
could have loved one another all along.

Wherein I Get Sick

Beware the Ides of March, the soothsayer says.
Beware the fever & the fret, the dry cough
from deep inside the cavern of your chest.
Your sense of taste dull, your sense of smell lost.
Chills rattle your bones & your useless teeth,
even as you lie buried beneath
blankets, duvets, the afghan your aunt made
for your wedding day forty years gone,
your red sheets wet with your own cold sweat.
Beware the most notorious of days.
As spring unfolds, as the light grows long,
fight for your breath & refuse crude death
who will take six hundred today.
Send the bastard on his way.

St. Patrick's Day

Damp drizzly March morning, a fit feast for
St. Patrick. Midway between Ash & Easter,
the world is Lenten weary. We want sun
every day when rain alone will do.
Less is ever more. A lesson that you
know to be true and yet refuse. It's no fun
to fast, stay indoors, abstain from little joys,
wine, chocolate, good bread, your daily run.
Like a child blessed with many toys
you cast your eye about and can't choose one.
You know in your bones that your own sweet breath
is all that spares you from your own sweet death.
The virus stalks you. A dagger unsheathing.
Less is always more. You keep on breathing.

My First Day Fever-Free

What happened to Day #7?
It was what stood between me
and 8, 9, 10, 11.
I spent it trying to see
the small buds break open
on our Black Cherry Tree.
It was a day given
to easy lethargy,
to slow naps and sudden
bouts of energy.
I was not driven.
I was my own entity.
I was forgiven
by the phlox, shriven by the bee.

A Psalm

"To be spiritual is to be amazed."

—Rabbi Abraham Joshua Heschel

I am amazed by the rain.
The way it falls upon us all,
the beautiful, the vain,
the outsized, the small.
I am amazed by the sun,
by its nightly departure,
by its daily return,
by its splendor & ardor.
I am amazed by my heart.
How it beats all night long,
never stops or departs
from its constant song.

My hands, my eyes, my tongue, amaze me,
as does the one who fearfully made me.

Survival

"The only way to fight the plague is with decency."

—Albert Camus, *The Plague*

Decency, meaning *seemliness*,
meaning *doing the right thing*,
meaning *fittingly* & *fittingness*,
meaning *becoming* & then *being*
the best soul you can be,
meaning *tend the sick*, *feed the hungry*,
open the door of your shut heart,
meaning *gentleness* & *modesty*
where compassion starts,
meaning *give it all away*,
every thing you've never wanted.
Resign yourself and stay
in place. Do not be haunted
by what's lost. Meaning *live undaunted*.

Super Moon

Last night we walked along the river path.
The full moon rose and shone its pale light
across the water. It did not feel like night
but, rather, evening or morning or something
in between, blue and smoky, like the last
set of a Jazz Man's song. What could go wrong
on a night like that? The sick & suffering
lay a few hundred yards from where we walked,
the hospital windows just out of view.
For now the world was just me and you.
We strolled slowly, eyed the sky and talked
of stars, how far they were and how long
it took their light to reach our river path,
how long after it dies a star's light lasts.

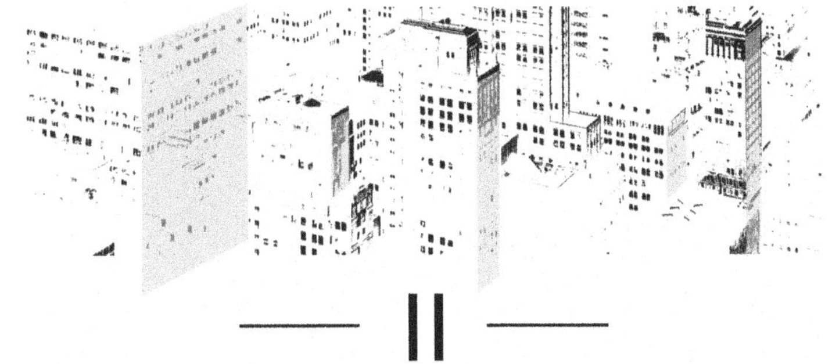

— II —

Palm Sunday

Christ rides into Jerusalem
but no one's there to see.
The donkey steps his way through town.
The streets are empty.
No palms wave as he passes by
the shut and shuttered shops.
He hears a distant baby cry.
The wayward donkey stops

to nose the stones beneath his feet
in search of grass or feed.
Christ calls, but there's no crowd to greet.
A shepherd without sheep.
No friends. No plotting enemies.
Christ rides through town, alive and free.

Good Friday

This good day dawns spectacular,
a red kiss from a red sky.
The world pursues its secular
desires. As if Christ did not die
for them today and not today
two thousand years ago. God walks
his way to Golgotha, past cars
and coffee shops. No one mocks
the man with the cross in his hand.
No one talks of three bright stars
that blaze on the horizon, a sign
of what's to come. Who can blame them?
Today is just another day.
Christ dies and loves us anyway.

Holy Saturday

It's Saturday and the wide world waits
for Christ to waken.
He died Good Friday afternoon
and left his good friends shaken.
They don't believe he will rise soon,
these men of little faith,

but we know better, living now,
his great feat did & done.
We know when & we know how
he'll rise before the sun,
walk the garden, speak to Mary,
do all that is necessary
to keep his promise, tried & true,
to them, to her, to me & you.

Easter

Joy is the Son & joy is my heart
this rising Easter morning.
The sun comes, the clouds part,
the small birds adorning
their nests with twigs & ribbon,
a bed to rest their eggs.
The gift we've been given,
new life. We watch the dregs
of winter poured out upon
the greening ground. Now done
is the rule of death & dearth.
Each seed & every creature of earth,
tired of the cold, tired of the night,
splits wide open & welcomes the light.

My Covid Birthday

Daylight dawns. So it has begun.
A day I thought would never come.

Fitting there should be wind & rain.
I'll never be 50 again.

Or 40, or 30, or 5, or 10.
And yet my body is the same

one I walked to school with, tanned
by the sea, ran and danced

with, taught how to be
quick on her feet, always hungry

for what life served up on a plate.
Like a good girl I always ate

what was set in front of me.
I'm done with that now. Welcome 60.

Wherein I Miss My Children

What divides us is just a few miles,
roadways & bridges, a river or two,
air & water, concrete & green trees.
March's wild gives way to April's mild,
the sun brings spring's reprieve,
and I am full of longing for you,
my doves, the three I gave birth to
on spring days not so far away.
Years have passed, a decade or two.
What binds us still we never say.
Call it habit, loyalty, love.
Whatever it is I dream of
mending this space that keeps us apart,
holding you in my arms as well as my heart.

The Ancients

At least it's not a plague that kills our children.
The one that broke a pharaoh long ago.
The one that Herod visited on inno-
cents. And there was the Pied Piper's grim
trick. The theft of young ones robs us of
our hope, marks & murders what we most love.

Our current plague is hungry for the old.
It ravages our present and our past.
The history they carry, the tales untold,
their witness to the fact that nothing lasts.
We can do without them, some say
as they die in dread numbers each day.

They have been our parents for so long.
Who will love us when they are all gone?

The Sea

"Only the sea, murmurous behind the
dingy checkerboard of houses,
told of the unrest, the precariousness,
of all things in this world."

—Albert Camus, *The Plague*

The sea knows, as does the river that feeds it,
as does the fish that glides within the heave
of every breaking wave. As does the osprey
who hovers high above the leaping fish,
the hunt for prey marking another day,
as does the sun that rules, the moon that reigns,
the mother of all waters: Nothing lasts
beyond the moment you perceive it.
The light you tried to paint already changed
before your brush touched the canvas.
Your face has aged. You do not look the same
as you did last year, last week, yesterday.
The body knows, the truth told by its bones.
The heart denies it, a sea of hope inside it.

Cabin Fever

I want to go to the beautiful places
I've gone with you before. To see the sea
from the cliffs of Sorrento, our balcony
blooming with orange blossoms, bodacious
Bougainvillea. To go back to Sicily,
to Etna's fiery dream. I am voracious
for sapphire skies, butter sun, the lovely
lift of light on water, long delicious
days of champagne & Sacher Torte, coffee
in Vienna, click of the white dishes,
cups, and spoons amid the noisy café.
If brute desire were efficacious,
love, it would transport us, just we,
from this gray prison to the blue blue sea.

In Which I Consider My Wardrobe

Six pairs of boots lined up in a row.
Three black suits hung limp in the closet.
Five idle dresses on the bedroom doors.
Eight earrings paired on the bureau top.
Leotards dangle from the doorknobs.
Silk scarves spread across the backs of chairs.
Like a used clothier peddling her wares
I could sell it all and never miss it.
How high my hopes when I bought each thing.
Admiring the make, modeling the fit.
Imagining where I would wear it.
A new pair of heels made my fool heart sing.
Little did I guess, little did I know
the pathos of clothes when there's no place to go.

Longing

"My salad days, when I was green in judgment."

—Shakespeare, *Antony & Cleopatra*

Now it begins to get stale.
Bread sitting on the shelf too long.
An egg just past its due date
smelling funky and strong.
My tongue craves what is fresh,
peaches picked from a real tree,
the sweet flesh of fruitness
slides down so easily.
Instead we eat what's dead,
thick meats, thicker gravy,
our hearts and our heads
heavy with dread,
appraising Cleopatra's phrase
longing for our salad days.

Shakespeare's 456th Birthday

A man who knew a thing or two about plague.
He survived it again and again.
Hic incepit pestis, three warning words
inked in the parish book after his birth,
then pursued him for all they were worth.
He knew himself lucky to be born in an age
of pestilence. Death's dreadful reign
killed people but could not kill art,
kindled the wood, threw off the spark
that sets every poet on fire.
Nothing is stronger than the desire
for life in the face of extremity.
The truth told in all of his poetry,
the cure he passed on to you and me.

Wherein I Teach Literature Remotely

The faces in the Zoom Room
look out at me from my computer screen,
each a little world made cunningly,
their beauty beyond telling. I see me,
too, a face among the faces, older,
lined by years theirs have not yet seen,
a sturdy face, one that has endured
time's slings & arrows. The future looms
ahead for us all, but especially
them, my students who will face disasters
unlike those I've seen. There is no cure
for it. We're all walking toward the tomb.
Shakespeare & Donne knew it. Now they do, too.
It breaks my heart when they sign off *Thank You.*

Our Emmaus

"And the two recounted what had taken place
on the way and how he was made known to them
in the breaking of the bread."

—Luke 24:35

You hand me the loaf, I tear off the heel,
dip it in the blue dish of olive oil—
this ritual performed at every meal
gladdens my heart. This is the real
presence of joy these days of pandemic.
The world's gone insane. People are frantic.
They talk of the news, the news, the news.

Terrible deaths. Bleak crucifixions.
Lives once well ordered now lack direction.
Better to sit here. Just me and you.
To set on our table olives and wine,
to savor the taste of sweet grapes and brine,
to raise our glasses and toast the poor dead,
to mend the world and to break our bread.

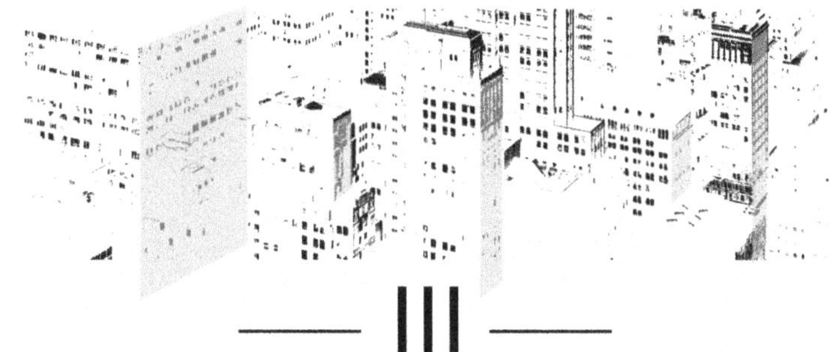

III

The Burial of the Dead

"Unreal City,
Under the brown fog of a winter dawn,
A crowd flowed over London Bridge, so many,
I had not thought death had undone so many."

—T. S. Eliot, "The Burial of the Dead," *The Wasteland*

They are digging mass graves on Hart Island.
No room enough to bury our dead
in the gentle places, the rolling green
spaces in Woodlawn, Brooklyn, where angels
keep watch, guardians of stone over fields
of bone. A sad chapter in our Novel
Virus story. Hart the final resting bed
of the indigent, despised, those who died
of AIDS, another plague that winnowed away
our faith in the body. How quickly it can
all go south. One day you're well, the next day
you are trucked to the Bronx to be buried.
They say the dead are many, the graves deep.
The digging does not disturb their sleep.

Here

What happened here could happen anywhere
there is love. So many people with so
many dreams. The old man who gave up his
breathing machine to the young man beside
him. The nurse who grieved him as he died.
The EMT who knelt beside the body
long after the heart had ceased to beat.
There are no more people on the street.
No friends going out for lunch or coffee.
So many people with no place to go.
No jobs, no plays, no films, no business
to tend to but hope in the midst of fear,
healing the world, every day a new prayer.
What happens here can happen anywhere.

The Virus Remakes the World

The animals are taking back the earth.
Birds build nests in the air conditioners.
Their hatchlings sing for all they're worth.
Deer in the back yard devour our flowers.
A brood of raccoon possess our garage.
Rats idle in our idle car engines.
The mice don't even try to camouflage
their comings & goings in our stocked cupboards.
The cats are taking multiple lovers
at night announcing their loud affections.
Our once-tame world slowly grows wild.
The being machines had long exiled
returns to regard us with curious eyes
and welcomes us into its paradise.

Four A.M.

The birds awoke before the birds awake
afraid they'll miss a moment of the day.
A brood to feed. A nest to make.
Light that comes is light that fades away.
My heart should take lessons from the birds.
She wakes and keeps the morning with them.
She has no hatchlings. All she owns is words,
the wayward hopes & hurts she herds & tends.
Night provides the soothing balm of grace,
a salve to wounds sustained in waking hours.
Only moon- and starlight can erase
the deep lines that score my aging face.
The birds don't care. They worship daylight's power.
So many chicks to raise. Worms to devour.

The Color of Covid

Gray the rain and gray the sky.
Gray the shade of Covid Spring.
The sun a myth. Warm and dry
the days that early May should bring.
The world is Lockdown Lead instead.
Heavy as a heartful of grief.
We rise up grateful we're not dead.
Yet the eye and the mind need relief
from the same pictures, the same dreams,
the same streets, the same scenes
enacted daily, the rituals
of food and sleep, habitual
rounds. Our lovely life grown plain.
The same gray sky. The same gray rain.

Locus Amoenus

"*Locus amoenus*, Latin for 'pleasant place,'
is a literary topos involving
an idealized place of safety or comfort."

—*Wikipedia*

Yesterday my loneliness struck full force,
a rogue wave of sadness caught me up
and pulled me out into a distant sea.
No fish were there, no birds of the air,
no good creature who could talk to me.
The land seemed far away, I felt remorse.
I missed the grit of sand beneath my feet.
I missed cafés, the friends I used to meet,
wine in our glasses, coffee in our cups,
the long conversations we would share.
I wondered if I'd ever be again
the girl I used to be back then.
I ate by the plateful, drank to the lees
the *locus* stretched out in front of me.

Relapse

I thought I had The Virus, but maybe not.
It seems the laugh is all on me.
The chills are back. My forehead raging hot.
I wake to find the world's calamity
lodged in my lungs, snaking down my throat,
living in my liver, a pleasure boat
rider hitchhiking through my bloodstream.
A nightmare and a fact that a being
so small can give birth to so much death,
can steal our freedom and can steal our breath.
It occupies our minds. It devours our dreams.
Nothing is as true or certain as it seems.
It tried to kill me once but could not best me.
Now it's back. Perhaps it never left me.

Covid Dreams

I've lost the infant again. Set him down
in some location I can't find. My mind
distracted by the doctor who asks me
questions I can't answer. I'm just the kind
of mom who misplaces her kids. *I see,*
he says, and then the baby is behind me,
facedown on a leather couch. He can't breathe.
I lift him up and am relieved. He's fine.
I'm on a hillside slowly sliding down.
An abyss yawns beneath. I grip the stone wall
as I slide by, which slides beside me. All
seems lost, then I see my grown son. I *know*
he will save me, grasp my hand. He says *no*.

Writing the Virus

The poems that come at night are full of blue.
My eye craves color when the world goes black.
My heart sings the sea. Dreams ensue.
I'm where I want to be and won't come back.
The day breaks blank and gray. I am awake.
My vivid Covid dreams don't come true.
(And I'm reminded, dreams never do.)
I rise late & lazy. Try to predict
the hours. No work. No job to go to.
Only the tasks my idle mind tricks
me into. Like this. I write for the sake
of the self I will be. She won't recall
the nights of blue longing. The gray dayfall.
Without me, she'll remember nothing at all.

Pandemic Acrostic

C is for Corona, the Queen
O f new disease, who gives the word
V irus a fresh sense of dread.
I is for me, this self that quarantine
D rives me indoors to live alone with.
1 is the number of times I've cried.
9 the number of times I've not died—

9 the number of lucky cats' lives,
1 the lucky number of mine.
D is for deaths others have died.
I was ill twice and survived.
V is for vincible, the myth
O f killing dead this Killer Queen.
C ure. There is none for Covid-19.

Sun Hunter

I've taken to chasing sunlight. The way
it spills across the page on the well-named
sunporch at seven a.m. And the way
it kindles the casement windows, framed
in dark oak at the back of the house, faced
east, at eight. And the way, by nine, it shines
hot and hard in my yard, setting the chaste
day on fire. And the way, by ten, it mends
my mood, assures me that we'll all be fine.
By noon I know light lies & dies. It sends
me out to run again, to seize the time
that flies again and perches in the trees.
At five it slants. My dumb heart grieves.
By nine it's gone. I'm on my knees.

The Race

The days run by, like horses out the gate.
Stamping and neighing, all at once it's eight
a.m. and another one's off, her mane on fire,
hoofs pounding the ground into dust,
her eight-pound heart full fueled by desire,
a hunger more urgent than any lust
a simple creature could know. Her legs say *go*
and cannot stop until the hours say so.
We are all whipped and driven by the clock,
more so than ever these pandemic days.
They fly by fast. Even as we are locked
in place, counting the minutes, counting the ways
to get from the start to the finish line,
we hear the hoofbeats keeping time.

May Song

Let there be flowers on all the tabletops,
lilacs & lilies, larkspur & rose.
Let there be birds in all the treetops,
robins & blue jays, finches & sparrows.
Open the windows to welcome their song,
to let in the breeze that blows sweet & long,
through the red maple, the cherry, the birch,
their branches clamoring with light & love,
days full of sunshine what they dream of
their deep months of sleep, heavy with snow.
Now is our moment. This is our earth.
No matter how leaden our hearts might be
let's lift them up. Let's let ourselves see
the courage of birds, each rose, every tree.

Wherein We Realize This is Not Temporary

"Thus the first thing that plague
brought to our town was exile."
—Albert Camus, *The Plague*

It was so lovely. We didn't even know it.
The place we were let to live each day.
Even if we knew it, we didn't show it.
Expectation & regret got in the way
of our seeing that life for the gift
it was. That was another country ago.
The train has left, all our money with it,
and we have arrived where we don't want to go.
We want to return to our city of love.
Our sweet celebrations all we think of
these days of lockdown and lonely exile.
They tell us it won't last. It's just for a while.
But we know better. The train's on the track.
It only runs forward. We'll never get back.

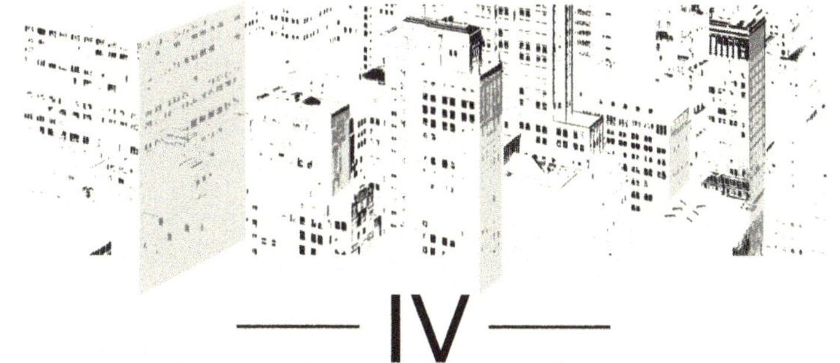

— IV —

Lockdown Metamorphosis

"*The Very Hungry Caterpillar* is a small, eccentric masterpiece—
a children's book, yes, but also a formative exploration
of the complex nature of change."
—*The New York Times*, May 24, 2020

Like the very hungry caterpillar
I shut myself up and became pure goo.
Evidently when they crawl in their cocoons
that's what very hungry caterpillars do.
I'm told this putrefaction that's occurred
will reverse and I will be made whole.
This slime become my eyes, this rank waste wings,
that I shall count among the lovely things
that grace the earth, though it's very slow.
I need to be patient and mark my time.
I begin to feel my antennae grow.
There's nothing less magical, less sublime,
more crass, more nasty, or more crude
than a butterfly with an attitude.

The Virus Begins to Abate

What is the music of late pandemic?
The birds that rise at four a.m.
The traffic lights that clunk & click.
The fall of footsteps on Macadam.
The wind in the rustling birch.
The riding mowers mowing grass.
The church bells in the empty church.
A lone car driving past.
The children's voices in the park.
The sudden silence after dark.
The slow & easy full moon night.
The pair of geese as they take flight.
The river rushing past the rocks.
The door at which no one knocks.

All Hallows Eve

October 31, 2020

First day of sun after three of rain.
The few leaves left shine with their own light.
All soon falls to the gravity of fall.
The shades of summer wander through our halls.
My bright dresses hang from the door frames,
my sandals arranged in a neat long line
waiting for the warm days to come again.
The windows are locked down, the house shut tight,
as if we could ward off what's out there.
Contagion rides on the cold blue air,
the curse of our era. Death comes to call
as a bat-borne virus, lethal and small.
We open our doors to the witches and ghosts
to welcome what comes, reluctant hosts.

Election 2020

Slip on your mask, button your coat.
Walk around the block to get your nerve.
Listen to the leaves drop from the trees
and skitter up the street. Round the curve,
turn the corner, pull your scarf round your throat.
Resist the urge to drop to your knees
and pray in the street as you prayed at home—
that you might right the world, that voting alone
might fix the future and mend the past.
You know the old story—nothing lasts,
the sorrow of the last four years will end.
Time is our enemy. Time is our friend.
We fill in the ballot. We feed the machine.
Hope where we're going is not where we've been.

Days of Hibernation

Now comes winter proper. Now's the time
for limb-rattling winds. The wild vine
that climbs the sleeping maple sleeps, too.
We alone awake, my love, just us two,
to watch the sun set the sky on fire,
to watch the trees kindle like tinder, admire
the way that noon slides slowly into night,
the way the icy river catches the light
and flings it back to the uncaring air.
We are hungry for it, here where
we have feasted for too long in the dark,
here where fear and pandemic leave their mark
on every human mind and human heart,
where getting through each day becomes an art.

Resurgence

Thanksgiving, November 26, 2020

After brief sleep, the pandemic is back,
roaring through the country, a hungry beast
who napped too long and needs to feed its fire.
All the signs are grim, the warnings dire.
Some will be the feasters, some the feast.
Dark winter falls on us and shades to black.
Gone our summer days, our summer haze
when we played like fools, like we'd escaped
the claw and maw of this unfettered eater.
Nothing more savory, nothing sweeter
than thinking we'd outwitted death for once,
deluded hope. Now he's back, now he hunts,
as we gather round our tables, wary
where we used to be so merry.

Indoor Exercise

Last night I tripped in my living room
while race-walking through the house
afraid of the virus outside,
the unkind cold, the treacherous ice.
Rounding the corner past the brown couch
for perhaps the fiftieth time, I fell
full force, nose to the floor. Blood gushed,
a geyser sprung from my stunned face,
molten me raining on the knickknacks,
the coffee table, the Turkish rug.
It pooled in my red hands. No ice pack
could slow the flow. It hurt like hell
as I sat alone, a wounded fool
cradling my self as I clotted and cooled.

Pandemic Advent

These the short days of Advent. He's coming.
He's got to be. We are besieged by dark-
ness. It falls on us an endless rain.
Sickness spreading like river water rising
and rushing past us. Some of us are marked
out for death and loss, circled by the pen
of contagion on Covid's graph of grief.
Some of us, unfairly, will stay safe,
hunched up in our houses, hatches battened
down, seemingly impervious, while the drowned
drift by, bodies bound for undug graves.
We count them instead of saying their names.
There are so many. Their faces hard to see.
We know He's coming. He's got to be.

Pandemic New Year

December 31, 2020

Time to say *goodbye, good luck,*
pack the old year's last lunch,
put on its mittens, tuck
that stray lock behind its ear once
more and no more. It's time
to board the bus to nowhere,
call a cab, catch a train
to anywhere that's not here.
We don't know where you're going
and we don't really care.
A new year is showing
up soon. We can bare-
ly contain our hoping & dreaming,
our glad sorry ache that you are leaving.

Pandemic Epiphany

January 6, 2021

So they've set out, despite the dire warnings.
The plague still raging, they have to travel light.
No entourage of jugglers, long slow mornings
of breakfast with tea and cake and spice.
Quick-made bread, cold meat will have to do,
chewed furtively beneath their scarves and masks.
No one questions, no one ever asks.
They pack up and go in search of You.

The roads are empty. The hospitals are full.
The world is sick, as it had always been.
The days are hot, the nights long and cool.
They ache to sleep in their own beds again.
Still they persist, those three holy men.
They'll quarantine when they get to Bethlehem.

The Doubts

Here they come again, cavorting before
me, like schoolkids waiting to be fed.
I break out the juice boxes, granola
bars, pass them around. One more encore
performance I dutifully do and I dread.
Corona, corona, corona
is all they buzz about, from the time
I rise till it's time to go to bed.
They grow fat on the *New York Times*,
gorge themselves on the *Washington Post*,
devour all the tweets, the President's lies
before I've finished my coffee and toast.
They nag me all day. I tell them it's fine.
I wish they were anyone else's but mine.

Confession

What do you expect? Admit it.

- Days without end.
- Joy unstopping.
- Not a single friend
- will die. No sibling.
- Certainly no child.

The world is a wild
beast. I know it.

- And yet I don't believe
  it will kill me.
- Somehow some reprieve
  will save me
  from its maw and save my loves, too.

- To die surprised that none of these are true.

Wherein I Await Vaccination

March 15, 2021
Bronx, New York

I stand in line with two hundred people.
We all wear masks, keep six feet apart.
We shuffle down the long hall, step squarely
in the small circle, the X that marks our spot.
After a year, we've been trained to stop
and stay in place until the line starts
to pull us along to the next marked circle.
Dante would approve. We move passively,
each station on the march its own little hell.
We're parts in the machine deftly designed
to circumscribe the virus. We are resigned
to this geometry. We can barely recall
the outlaw handshakes, hugs we dearly miss,
the human smile, the forbidden kiss.

Anniversary

March 22, 2021

A year since the lockdown and we're still here,
poking our heads out the back door,
scant scent of snowdrops in the air,
blinking our eyes in the cold sun.
A year of privation has gone and come,
living with less, starving for more,
we venture out this vaccine spring
full of slow hope the pandemic's done.
No Times Square kisses. No bells will ring
announcing our ordeal is over.
Just the tentative step, the listening
for the crack in the ice, the inkling
that the world will once more hold our weight.
For too many it comes too late.

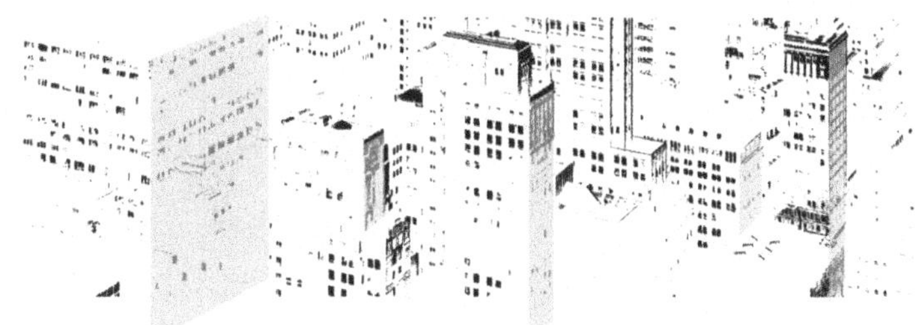

EPILOGUE

Pandemic Prayer

Bless the day that dawns on us.
        We are in need of light.
Bless the birds that flit and fuss.
        They've been asleep all night.
Bless the cats who wear no masks
        slinking through the yard.
Bless the simple daily tasks
        that have become so hard
to do without—
                the fire pit's blaze,
        the meals I make with joy,
the windows that I wash and raise.
        The virus can't destroy
this urge to bless our life & praise
        even these pandemic days.

ALSO BY ANGELA ALAIMO O'DONNELL

Still Pilgrim
Poems

ISBN 978-1-61261-864-7
Trade paperback • $19

"If rhyme and meter are, as Heaney said, the table manners of the language arts, then Angela Alaimo O'Donnell has set out a sumptuous feast, if not bardic, then beatific, recalling a time when pilgrims knew to spread good word by heart." —**Thomas Lynch**, author of *Walking Papers* and *The Sin-eater: A Breviary*

Andalusian Hours
Poems from the Porch of Flannery O'Connor

ISBN 978-1-64060-353-0
Trade paperback • $19

"Get ready to delight in, yes, a full cento of gorgeous, endlessly fascinating and endlessly varied sonnets in a no-nonsense Georgia-bound idiom, this two-year labor of real love, where one of our best contemporary Catholic poets has managed—thank God—to channel the wit, humor, and profound spirituality of our own saint Flannery O'Connor, broken and flawed like the rest of us, whether we know it or not, and yet risen now once again in these poems and crying out, startling us into a brilliant new reality, like one of those blue peacocks of hers unfolding a hundred eyes before us." —**Paul Mariani**, author of *The Mystery of It All: The Vocation of Poetry in the Twilight of Modernity*

Available at bookstores
Paraclete Press • 1-800-451-5006 • www.paracletepress.com